About the Author™

Meet

Jane Yolen

Alice B. McGinty

The Rosen Publishing Group's
PowerKids Press™
New York

To Jane

Published in 2003 by The Rosen Publishing Group, Inc.
29 East 21st Street, New York, NY 10010

Copyright © 2003 by The Rosen Publishing Group, Inc.

All rights reserved. No part of this book may be reproduced in any form without permission in writing from the publisher, except by a reviewer.

First Edition

Editor: Frances E. Ruffin
Book Design: Maria E. Melendez

Photo Credits: Cover, title page, pp. 20, 21, 22 © Jason Stemple; pp. 2, 3, 4, 5, 7, 9, 10, 11, 15 courtesy of Jane Yolen; pp. 8 (top), 19 (top) Maura B. McConnell; pp. 12, 14 David Stemple, courtesy of Jane Yolen; p. 16 © 1999 Erin Gristead, courtesy of Jane Yolen.

Grateful acknowledgment is made for permission to reprint previously published material:
p. 8 (bottom): From MIZ BERLIN WALKS by Jane Yolen, illustrated by Floyd Cooper, copyright © 1997 by Floyd Cooper, illustrations. Used by permission of Philomel Books, an imprint of Penguin Putnam Books for Young Readers, a division of Penguin Putnam, Inc.
p. 19 (bottom): From OWL MOON by Jane Yolen, Illustrated by John Schoenherr, copyright © 1987 by John Schoenherr, illustrations. Used by permission of Philomel Books, an imprint of Penguin Putnam Books for Young Readers, a division of Penguin Putnam, Inc.

McGinty, Alice B.
  Meet Jane Yolen / Alice B. McGinty.— 1st ed.
      p. cm. — (About the author)
  Summary: A short biography of Jane Yolen, a prolific and well-known writer of juvenile literature.
  Includes bibliographical references and index.
  ISBN 0-8239-6407-8 (library binding)
  1. Yolen, Jane—Juvenile literature. 2. Authors, American—20th century—Biography—Juvenile literature. 3.
  Children's literature—Authorship—Juvenile literature. [1. Yolen, Jane. 2. Authors, American. 3. Women—Biography.]
    I. Title. II. Series.
    PS3575.O43 Z77 2002
      813'.54—dc21

                                       2002000116

Manufactured in the United States of America

Contents

Worlds upon a Windowsill

There once was a little girl who liked to sit curled up on a window seat facing New York's Central Park. As she sat, she read. Jane Yolen read **folktales** and fairy tales. She read about the **legendary** King Arthur and Robin Hood. Jane's reading took her far from New York City, to worlds filled with magic and wonder. The tales she read became part of her, and when Jane grew up, she wrote tales of her own. Her stories are filled with dragons, **wizards**, heroes and heroines, magic, adventure, and wonder. Having written more than 250 books, Jane Yolen is known as one of the greatest storytellers of our time.

◄ Left: *As a young girl, Jane lived in New York City.*

Five-year-old Jane sat for this picture with her brother Steven, who is three years younger.

The "Write" Family

While living in Virginia, Jane and her cousin Michael watched ships that sailed from the Chesapeake Bay. These ships were taking soldiers to Europe to fight in World War II. Sometimes Jane and Michael waded in the dirty, oily water of the bay. Jane later turned memories of these visits into a book called All Those Secrets of the World.

Jane Hyatt Yolen was born on February 11, 1939, in New York City. Writing and storytelling were part of her family's history. Jane's great-grandfather had been a storyteller in his Ukrainian village. Jane's father, Will, had been a **journalist**. He had also been the world's kite-flying champion and wrote books about kite flying. Jane's mother, Isabelle, had been a **social worker** and a writer. She left social work to raise Jane and Steven, Jane's younger brother. When Jane was four, she watched her father sail away in a large ship. He was going to fight in **World War II**. While her father was gone, Jane, her mother, and her brother lived with her grandparents in Virginia.

Jane's family loved music. One-and-a-half-year-old Jane is shown in this photo with her mother and father, who played the guitar and sang folk songs.

"There was feathers to the right
and feathers to the left,
tickling my nose,
and falling on Bubba's head."
I finished my ice cream
and wiped my sticky hands
on my flower sunsuit.
Without missing a step,
without missing a word,
she reached back
and grabbed hold of my hand,
threading her fingers through mine.
We walked side by side then,
her telling more of the tale.
"So there I was in the creek, child.
Some of those feathers,
they were dove gray.
And some were crow black.
And some were dirty white,
like seagulls after the swill.
But one rained right into my hand,
and it was all over gold."

King Arthur

Jane's father returned home at the end of the war. The family moved back to New York City, and Jane began first grade. When Jane read the whole first-grade reading book in one night, her teacher moved her straight to the second grade. That year, Jane wrote the words and music for a class musical. Everyone played a vegetable. Jane was the lead carrot! When she was eight, Jane discovered stories about King Arthur in an **encyclopedia** at home and found more books about him at the public library. She turned the stories into games. She made her brother, Steven, and her best friend, Diane, play evil characters, while Jane played the heroes.

◀ *The idea for Jane's book,* Miz Berlin Walks, *came from seeing her grandmother, Fanny Berlin, take evening walks around the block.*

This is a photo of Jane at age five. When she was 13 years old, her family moved from New York City to Westport, Connecticut.

Growing Up

Jane grew up singing, dancing, reading, and writing. She took ballet lessons and dreamed with friends about life as a dancer. Jane enjoyed writing schoolwork in **rhyme**.

After Jane graduated from high school in 1956, she attended Smith College in Massachusetts. She studied religion and **literature**, including the tales of King Arthur. While attending college, Jane also wrote poems. Many of Jane's poems won awards. Jane graduated from Smith College in 1960. After graduation, Jane's boyfriend asked her to marry him. Instead, she chose to move back to New York City. She told him, "I have to find out if I can be a writer."

Jane had many friends at Staples High School in Westport, Connecticut. She became the captain of the girls' basketball team, even though she was the shortest player.

Jane and Mike Lieber, her singing partner, teamed up as a singing act during their college days. ▶

The Letter

In New York, Jane worked for several literary magazines and helped her father to write a book about kite flying. One day an **editor** from a big **publisher** wrote to Jane, asking if she was writing a book at that time. Jane's college professor had told the editor that Jane was a talented writer. Jane was not writing a book at that time. She had an idea for one about lady pirates, but the editor was not interested in Jane's idea. Jane then visited a publisher her father knew. That editor told Jane she would consider her book idea about pirates. Two months later, on Jane's twenty-second birthday, the editor offered Jane a **contract** to write *Pirates in Petticoats*.

Jane Yolen shares this advice with young writers, "Read, read, read! You must read every day, and try to read a wide range of books. Write, write, write! Keep a journal, write letters, anything to keep the 'writing muscles' in shape. Don't let anyone stop you from writing."

This 1960s photo shows Jane with a statue of Hans Christian Andersen, who wrote fairy tales. Jane is called the American Hans Christian Andersen.

Going Places

Jane met David Stemple in 1960, when he climbed through a window to get into a crowded party that Jane and her friends had given. Jane and David soon fell in love. They were married in 1962. David worked with computers and was a photographer. Working as an assistant editor at A. A. Knopf, Jane continued to write stories. She sent them to publishers, but they didn't buy her stories. In 1964, Frances Keene, editor in chief for the children's book department of Macmillan, published Jane's funny fairy tale, *The Witch Who Wasn't*. In 1965, Jane and David quit their jobs. They traveled around Great Britain, France, Greece, and Israel in a V W camper. Their travels offered good research for Jane's writing.

This photograph of Jane was taken by David in 1960, before they were married.

Jane and David were photographed while traveling out West in the 1970s. ▶

jane yolen

A photo of a Stemple family gathering during Christmas 1999 shows Jane and David and their family, including their grandchildren.

A Growing Family

When Jane and David returned from their travels in 1966, they moved to Massachusetts, where David found a job in the computer center at the University of Massachusetts. Soon after they had moved, Jane gave birth to their daughter, Heidi Elisabet. More good things were happening for Jane as well. Three more of Jane's books were purchased by publishers and would be printed.

Jane stayed at home to raise Heidi. In the years that followed, Jane wrote many stories and gave birth to two sons, Adam and Jason. Jane and David bought a 14-room farmhouse in the small town of Hatfield, Massachusetts, for their family.

Jane has always kept busy. Besides being a mother, she wrote her books, organized writers' groups and conferences, and earned her master's degree in education from the University of Massachusetts.

Winning Awards

By the 1980s, many children and adults had fallen in love with Jane's books. Her books have won many awards. In 1988, her book *Owl Moon* won the Caldecott Medal that is given to the best picture book. In Jane's novel, *The Devil's Arithmetic*, a girl travels back in time to the **Holocaust**. The book won many awards. Jane also twice won the Nebula Award given by the Science Fiction and Fantasy Writers of America, and the Golden Kite Award given by the Society of Children's Book Writers and Illustrators for *The Girl Who Cried Flowers and Other Tales*. In 2000, Jane won the Christopher Medal from the Christopher Society for *How Do Dinosaurs Say Goodnight?*

"Our feet crunched over the crisp snow and little gray footprints followed us.
Pa made a long shadow, but mine was short and round.
I had to run after him every now and then to keep up, and my short, round shadow bumped after me.
But I never called out. If you go owling you have to be quiet, that's what Pa always says.
I had been waiting to go owling with Pa for a long, long time."
—from Owl Moon
(1997)

A page from Owl Moon is shown here. The idea for the book came after her husband, David, took their daughter, Heidi, owling.

Pa turned on
his big flashlight
and caught the owl
just as it was landing
on a branch.

Phoenix Farm

At her farmhouse, which she calls Phoenix Farm, Jane's two workrooms in her attic are lined with books. For nine years she directed a publishing **imprint** called Jane Yolen Books. Jane's husband, David, is the first person to read her new stories. Jane's daughter Heidi writes books with Jane. Her son Jason takes photographs for some of her books, and her son Adam is a musician and helps Jane to write songs. Sometimes Jane sings with Adam's band. Jane also spends time with her three grandchildren. Jane and her family enjoy spending summers in St. Andrews, Scotland.

◀ Award-winning author Jane Yolen, shown working at her computer, has said that her best award is when a child loves her books.

Jane says she has enough story ideas to keep her writing for the rest of her life and longer, if she could. She wants to keep writing so that she can continue to pass the wonder and magic of her stories on to others.

In Her Own Words

When did you know that you wanted to be a writer?
Both my parents were writers so I assumed, from the time I understood what writing was, that *all* adults are writers. I also wanted to be, at various times, a ballet dancer, a horse trainer, and a lawyer.

What do you enjoy best about your job?
Finding out how a new story ends!

What kind of research do you do for your books?
I do lots and lots and lots. I am *always* researching. I read histories and **biographies** . . . folktales, bird books, and plant books, and flower books, and books about jewels. I am a researching fool.

How do you choose your topics?
My topics seem to choose me.

What impressions would you like readers to take away from your books?
I want my readers to love the story and walk away saying, "That story feels as if it has been around forever and yet it is somehow brand new, too." I want my readers to be changed for the good by my stories. As one little boy wrote to me, "Your stories will live forever. I hope you live to 99 or 100 but who cares." Who cares, indeed!

For Jane, the best awards are when children love her books.

Glossary

biographies (by-AH-gruh-feez) Books that give a history of people's lives.

contract (KAHN-trakt) An agreement, usually written, between two or more people.

editor (EH-dih-ter) The person who corrects errors, checks facts, and decides what will be printed in a newspaper, book, or magazine.

encyclopedia (in-sy-kluh-PEE-dee-uh) A book that has information about a wide range of subjects, usually in alphabetical order.

folktales (FOHLK-taylz) Stories that have been handed down among people.

Holocaust (HAH-luh-kost) The mass murder of millions of Europeans, especially Jewish people, by Nazis during World War II.

imprint (IM-print) A separate section of a larger publishing house.

journalist (JER-nuhl-ist) A person who gathers, writes, and presents news for a newspaper, magazine, or television program.

legendary (LEH-jen-der-ee) To be famous and important.

literature (LIH-tuh-ruh-chur) The writings of a certain country or period of time.

publisher (PUH-blih-shur) A person or company whose business is printing and selling books, newspapers, or magazines.

rhyme (RYM) Using words that, at the end, sound like other words.

social worker (SOH-shul WERK-uhr) A person who works with people who have problems and who helps them to improve their lives.

wizards (WIH-zerdz) People with magical powers.

World War II (WURLD WOR TOO) A war that was fought by many countries of the world from 1939 to 1945.

Index

Web Sites

Due to the changing nature of Internet links, PowerKids Press has developed
an online list of Web sites related to the subject of this book. This site is
updated regularly. Please use this link to access the list:
www.powerkidslinks.com/aa/janeyol/